THE
Archive Photographs
SERIES

SAAB
AIRCRAFT

Saab 91 Safir trainers of the Swedish Air Force when they entered service in 1952. Here eight Safirs fly in stepped-up echelon formation.

THE
Archive Photographs
SERIES

SAAB
AIRCRAFT

Compiled by
Derek N. James

*Published to mark the 60th Anniversary of the founding of Svenska Aeroplan
Aktiebolaget (SAAB).*

CHALFORD

First published 1997
Copyright © Derek N. James, 1997

The Chalford Publishing Company
St Mary's Mill, Chalford,
Stroud, Gloucestershire, GL6 8NX

ISBN 0 7524 1080 6

Typesetting and origination by
The Chalford Publishing Company
Printed in Great Britain by
Bailey Print, Dursley, Gloucestershire

For all those who, during the last sixty years, have helped to build Saab's reputation for exciting, innovative and effective aeroplanes.

Till alla dem som under de senaske 60 åren har hjälpt till att bygga upp Saab:s rykte som tillverkare av spannande, nyskapande och effektiva flygplan.

By the same author
Bristol Aeroplane Company
Dowty and the Flying Machine
Gloster Aircraft Company
Hawker Aircraft
Westland Aircraft

Other titles in the Archive Photographs Aviation Series
Air Transport: The First Fifty Years
Avro Aircraft
Blackburn Aircraft
Boulton Paul Aircraft
De Havilland Aircraft
Fairey
Filton and the Flying Machine
Hendon to Farnborough SBAC Displays 1932 -1975
Junkers
Napier Powered
Percival Aircraft
Staffordshire and Black Country Airfields
Shorts Aircraft
Supermarine
Vickers

in preparation
Armstrong Whitworth *Messerschmidt*
Cobham PLC *Miles*
Croydon Airport *Saunders-Roe*
Dornier *Sopwith*
Handley Page

Contents

Acknowledgements

Some 2,500 years ago Confucius, the philosopher, discovered the value of pictures in books. He actually equated their value. 'One picture is worth a thousand words'. He said it in Chinese, of course, because his real name was K'ung-fu-tse which means K'ung the Master. If he got his sums right, then without its 211 photographs, this book would have been three times its present size.

That is why I owe a great debt of gratitude to Anders Annerfalk, Saab's Vice President-Communications and Public Affairs and to Mike Hooks, the renowned aviation author. Anders unearthed a wealth of unusual and unpublished photographs of Saab aircraft, his interest in aviation history clearly guiding his choice of subjects. Mike's photo-archives seem bottomless, as is his generosity in lending photographs to we who write. Because of their antiquity, many of the photographs were uncaptioned and required a great deal of bi-national sleuthing for clues to the identity of people and events. Without the help and encouragement of Mike Savage, Saab Aircraft International's Vice President-Public Relations and Promotional Services, this book would not have got off the ground and I am most grateful to him for all that he did for me. Catherine Fraccia, Mike's most efficient secretary, has helped me in many ways and I thank her for her cheerful and ready assistance.

During a visit to Linköping I was privileged to meet a number of Saab executives: Ulf Edlund, Vice President-Strategic Planning; Michael Ehrenborg, Director-Market Analysis; Stig Holmström, Sales Executive and former chief test pilot; Lars Jansson, Manager-Communications and Public Affairs; Per-Olof Otterström, Vice President-Government Programmes. All spared time in their busy day to answer questions and brief me on Saab products, people and events. Anita Neuman, Press Assistant at the Embassy of Sweden, London, responded instantly to my request for a translation of this book's dedication into Swedish. They contributed much to this Saab story and I am deeply grateful to them.

Although this is an aviation book, for many people the name Saab means motorcars. It is fifty years since the first Saab motorcar was built. Thus, the book contains photographs of some Saab cars and I thank Joanne Cox, Saab GB's Public Relations Assistant who provided them.

My thanks go to Alan Sutton, David Buxton, Fionn O'Toole, Simon Thraves and Virginia Willcox of Chalford Publishing Company for their support in creating this book. As ever, the intuitive mastery of our PC and its software by my wife, Brenda, and her endless patience, has made intelligible the work of my faltering fingers on the same keyboard and prepared it for the publishers.

Finally, congratulations to Saab! May the next sixty years be as stimulating for us and as rewarding for the Company as the sixty which have preceded them.

Derek N. James,
Barnwood,
Gloucester.
September 1997

One

SAAB

As it was in the Beginning

The four capital letters in the above title, which was the original name of the Company, stand for Svenska Aeroplan Aktiebolaget AB, which takes up a lot of space on paper and is a bit tiresome to repeat too often! So how to shorten and spell it? SAAB? SAAB Aktiebolaget? Saab Aircraft? Let's go for Saab which, since the mid-1960s with a few additions, has been the officially accepted style of writing the name of this great and unique Swedish company. On second thoughts, perhaps really it should be Saab-Scania, but as this name was not sanctioned by Sweden's National Patent and Registration Office until 8 June 1970, ie. for less than half of the Company's sixty years, we'll stick to the universally known and used name: Saab.

Write it how you will, this name instantly produces a mental picture of a company which seems to have produced every one of Sweden's aeroplanes, most of their equipment, plus the majority of its private and commercial motor vehicles. Not wholly true. It may come as a surprise to many readers to know that before Saab, which was formed in April 1937, there had been some fifteen previous Swedish organisations in the aircraft business. Identified by bewildering groups of capital letters (SW, SAF, NAB, ASJA... the list goes on) they built French, Dutch, German, US and British aeroplanes and engines under licence.

By 1917 the first three companies to be formed had closed their doors for the last time and the fourth, AB Enoch Thulin Aeroplan Fabrick (founded in 1913 by Dr E. Thulin, Sweden's pioneer aviator and aircraft industrialist) followed suit a year after he was killed in a flying accident on 14 May 1919.

Two other companies are of particular interest. Svenska Aero AB, formed in 1921 and AB Flygindustri, established four years later, were virtually shadow 'subsidiaries' for the Heinkel and Junkers organisations respectively. This ruse enabled these German firms to maintain their aircraft design and manufacturing skills in Sweden while prohibited from doing so in their own country by the Versailles Treaty. (Money problems would sink Svenska Aero AB in 1932 and it would be bought by AB Svenska Järnsvägsverkstäderna - ASJ, while AB Flygindustri would put up the shutters in 1935, its German design staff returning to the Fatherland.)

Hitherto, Sweden's air defences had been in the hands of the Army Air Corps and the Naval Air Service, the former building some aircraft in its own workshops while the Navy imported foreign types. Then, in 1925, Sweden's Government amalgamated these two Services and formed an autonomous Swedish Air Force - *Flygvapnet* - which will be referred to as SwAF. (A separate Army Aviation was again created in 1954 followed by Naval Aviation three years later). During the next decade many of its aircraft were licence-built. It was not until 1936 that an indigenous aircraft industry was deemed a viable project. A number of Swedish engineering companies began examining the possibility of building aircraft; among them was ASJ which had an aircraft subsidiary. This was AB Svenska Järnvägsverkstäderna Aeroplanavdelning - ASJA. Bofors, the big armaments company with its subsidiary Nohab Flygmotorfabriker, was able to offer a complete package of facilities (but not a lot of experience) for airframe, engine, weapons and equipment design and production. Attractive as this appeared, the SwAF procurement experts who were, in principle, in favour of competitive bids from manufacturers, could not lightly dismiss ASJA's long experience in airframe design and manufacture. Neither could they afford to support two major manufacturers. Bofors suggested an amalgamation of the two organisations but the response by ASJA was firmly 'negative'. However, in March 1937 after some lengthy commercial, financial and political 'jousting', they both agreed to create a joint management and development company to rationalise design and administration and to allocate orders. Named AB Förenade Flygverkstäder (AFF), it was soon in business. A few weeks later Bofors formed Svenska Aeroplan Aktiebolaget AB - SAAB, (from here onward the company will be referred to as Saab) and began building factories for this new company. So did ASJA at Linköping.

One of some thirty Heinkel He5 float planes licence-built as S5s by Svenska Aero for the Swedish Air Force (SwAF) during 1927-30. The pilot talks to uniformed personnel, who examine the floats, watched by surprised local farm workers in whose field the S5 has forced landed.

Saab licence-built sixteen German Junkers Ju86K bombers as B3s for the Swedish Air Force during 1938-40. With a 22.7 m (74 ft 6 in) wing span the B3 carried four crew and a 1,000 kg (2,204 lb) bomb load.

A civil-registered Junkers Ju86K, SE-CBO, converted to become a transport aircraft, seen at Bromma Airport, Stockholm.

The first of four Hawker Hart two-seat light bombers built for the Swedish Air Force and delivered in 1934. A total of forty-two Harts with 550 hp Nohab-built Bristol Pegasus IU2 engines were built by ASJA during 1935-36.

This ASJA Viking was re-engined with a 150 Czech Walter radial engine and was mounted on floats in about 1935. The 'S-T' marking on the rudder indicates that it was owned by *Stockholms -Tidningen* newspaper.

Two

Up the Learning Curve

Apart from the brief period of their accord during the formation of AFF, Saab and ASJA were in constant opposition, no more so than during early 1938 when both submitted design proposals for a reconnaissance/light bomber aircraft for close support of ground forces or maritime operations. The winner was the ASJA L-10 project. It would be produced, a year or so later, as the Saab 17!

The first aircraft ordered from this fledgling 'industry' were to be produced under licence from North American Aviation (NA-16 - 4M advanced trainers), Northrop Corporation (8A-1 single-engined dive bombers) and from Junkers (Ju86K twin-engined bombers). The orders, placed during late summer 1938, had been channelled through AFF which had allocated trainer and dive bomber production to ASJA with Saab getting the go-ahead to build the Ju86Ks.

It was becoming clear to the SwAF and the Government - each showing more than a hint of impatience - that the two companies could never work together. In December 1938 matters were taken out of their hands by AFF and its chairman Torsten Nothin. They were given a month to resolve their problems. In March 1939 Saab was completely reorganised and, effectively, took over ASJA to produce airframes. During the previous year Saab had begun employing numbers of specialist US designers and engineers. Thus their expertise and experience became available to Saab when it swallowed ASJA. But the learning curve had to become steeper if the production programmes for these advanced all-metal aircraft could be described as 'up-and-running'.

The first batch of Ju86Ks was assembled from German-made components and the first wholly Swedish-built example first flew during August 1939. A total of eighty were originally ordered, forty of them direct from Junkers Flugzeug AG and the remainder from Saab. However, the outbreak of the Second World War in September 1939 not only ended the planned imports from Germany, but this time it was the US technicians who were recalled home. By the time Saab had built sixteen Ju86Ks in January 1941, production ceased as this seven year old design was being swiftly outdated. However, a number of problems reared their ugly heads. They were mainly due to Saab's shortage of manpower with experience of designing and building advanced all-metal structures. To overcome these difficulties Saab launched a large training programme to produce the sort of technically-equipped people it sorely needed among its workforce.

Meanwhile, work on the B17 reconnaissance/light bomber which had begun with advice and assistance from the US engineers, moved ahead in Swedish hands led by Frid Wänström. Despite a temporary halt to this work lasting several months, the first one was flown by Claes Smith, Saab's chief test pilot, on 18 May 1940 - albeit with the retractable landing gear locked down. (Numbers of other prototypes around the world would make their first flights with their landing gear in a similar position) There was a white-knuckle moment for Smith when the long canopy over the two cockpits broke away in flight, but he made a safe landing after having his head battered from side to side by the slip-stream.

During the ensuing four years a total of two prototype L-10s and 322 B17 production aircraft were built in four sub-types. They equipped eighteen SwAF squadrons, which operated them on wheel and ski landing gear and on floats, powered either by Swedish-built 1,060 hp Pratt & Whitney Twin Wasps or 980 hp Bristol Mercuries, or by imported 1,080 hp Piaggio P.IX bis radial engines. The bomber variants were equipped with a unique bomb sight of Saab design which greatly improved the aircraft's operational effectiveness. B17s were exported in quantity for the Ethiopian Air Force - *Ye Ethiopia Ayer Hail* - where some served until the 1970s. Post-war, numbers were operated as target towers by Svenska Flygjänst and three were sold to Finland and Austria for the same task. Happily, the B17A, serialled 17329, which belongs to the Swedish Air Force Museum, has been restored to airworthiness by retired Saab and SwAF volunteers who have devoted some 7,000 hours of work to this task. It first flew again in mid June 1997.

While Saab had had the help of the US designers on the B17, the company's next aeroplane, for which initial design work began in 1939, was entirely Swedish. Originally ASJA's L-11 project, the work of Bror Bjurströmer, which was chosen in preference to two other projects submitted by Saab (prior to its acquisition of ASJA) and Gotäverken, this twin-engined aeroplane was designated B18. By early 1940 two prototypes had been ordered and soon metal was being cut. Due to the war a good deal of secrecy surrounded this aeroplane. When it was rolled out in May 1942 it showed a remarkable similarity to the renowned Dornier family of bombers then in service with the *Luftwaffe*.

Although the two prototypes and the first batch of B18As were scheduled to have licence-built 1,060 hp Pratt & Whitney Twin Wasp engines, it was realised even at the design stage that they would be under-powered; thus later production aircraft were intended to have the more powerful 1,300 hp Bristol Taurus engines. However, when plans to fit this British engine collapsed, an approach was made to Germany for a licence to build the 1,025 hp Daimler-Benz DB 601 in-line engine. Long negotiations failed. Then, out of the blue, in the summer 1941, the Germans offered the newer 1,450 hp DB605 instead! On 19 June 1942, the first prototype B18A got airborne to begin the lengthy flight development programme. First deliveries to the SwAF's F1 Wing based at Västerås began in March 1944. Just three months later the first DB605-powered B18B made its first flight.

During the next fifteen years B18 variants were continually modified as new equipment and systems became available. Among these were radar and camera installations for the S18A strategic reconnaissance aircraft, ejector seats, rocket projectiles and, in the T18B, the very heavy armament of a 57 mm and two 20 mm cannon which, allied to a 595 kph (370 mph) top speed, made this variant a formidable aeroplane indeed. A total of 244 B18s were built. The type flew with some eighteen squadrons, the last ones serving until early in 1959.

A Saab 17B with a 980 hp Swedish-built Bristol Mercury XXIV engine which exhausts over the wing. The very large main landing gear fairings could be used as air brakes when dive bombing.

Ten Swedish Air Force B17As, with 1,065 hp Pratt & Whitney Twin Wasp engines, ready for delivery. Most of the 322 B17s were built at the Trollhättan factory.

A trio of Swedish Air Force B17Bs with licence-built Bristol Mercury engines. The very long cockpit canopy provides a good all-round view for the two crew members.

With retractable skis replacing the wheeled landing gear and its bulky fairings, the B17B was a very clean fighter-like aeroplane.

A Mercury-powered B17BS on floats. Note the tailplane finlets to counter the float side area and the three steps on the float pylon's leading edge.

All jacked up and nowhere to go. This B17B on jacks is probably prepared for landing gear retraction tests - or, perhaps, for a publicity photograph!

Eighteen Saab 17As of the Imperial Ethiopian Air Force. As cockpits are open and the tyres are covered - possibly against the sun's heat - this photograph may have been taken at the IEAF's Asmara base.

This remarkable photograph shows Emperor Haile Selassie of Ethiopia in a cloak, with Colonel Count Gustaf von Rosen, who reformed the IEAF after the Second World War, behind him in the photograph. The Emperor leads members of the IEAF and his entourage after an inspection of recently arrived Saab 17s. A magnifying glass reveals that no one has looked up at the aircraft flying overhead!

The pilot of this B18A checks its Pratt & Whitney Twin wasp engines before flight. The twin fins and rudders, dihedral tailplane single leg landing gear and cockpits off-set to port are noteworthy.

The clean lines of this B18A are revealed in this side view. Its marked similarity to some of the German Dornier family of bombers is apparent, particularly the tail unit.

Photographed on its sunny side the B18A looks a pugnacious aeroplane.

Converted from the B18A bomber, this S18A strategic reconnaissance version carries a US-built radar in an under-fuselage pod. The S18A was the first radar-equipped Swedish Air Force aircraft.

18

While the crew of this S18A strategic reconnaissance aircraft read their briefing notes, we get a close up of its nose and radar pod - well, most of it. A prototype Lansen in this picture dates it about 1953.

Two SwAF S18As, one with its radar pod fitted, the other with engines running, stand on the snow-covered Luleå airfield.

B18Bs with 1,475 hp Daimler-Benz DB695B engines in final assembly. The heavily-framed windscreens and the tubular engine mountings cantilevered off the front wing spar are noteworthy.

The B18B was a menacing shape in the air. The attack variants had 1,475 hp Daimler-Benz DB605 in-line engines and twin ejector seats. They served with the SwAF from 1945 to 1958.

A SwAF armourer works on the big 5.3 m (17 ft 3 in) long 57 mm Bofors cannon in the nose of a T18B attack aircraft. The aperture for the starboard 20 mm cannon can also be seen.

The pilot of this T18B demonstrates his correct position for escaping from an aircraft in an emergency using the Saab ejection seat. He holds the firing cord in his right hand.

Three
Now for Some Things Different

The future development of military aircraft was an important feature of an agreement between the Swedish Government and aircraft industry drawn up in late 1940 to provide a sound basis on which the industry could depend when planning its expansion programmes. While the first two Saab designs had been for virtually multi-role aircraft able to undertake reconnaissance, bomber and attack missions, the company's project office had studied requirements for pure fighter aircraft.

It is recorded that as early as April 1941, Saab had produced a design, the L-21, for a twin-boom tricycle landing gear fighter with a pusher engine/propeller configuration. It is recorded that Frid Wänström took only ten days to complete the initial design. The engine was a Daimler- Benz DB605. This was an inspired piece of forward planning - or was it wishful thinking? At that time Germany was refusing to grant a licence to Sweden to produce the older and lower-powered DB601; negotiations for the licence to build the DB605 did not recommence until August or September. Happily, when they came to fruition, Saab was poised ready to proceed with final design work the moment it received the Air Board's go-ahead.

The unusual mounting of the power unit caused a number of problems, not least that of providing cooling air to the radiators on the ground when there was no propeller-generated air flow through them. Then there was the need for an effective pilot ejector seat system to carry him clear of the propeller in the event of an emergency ejection. Minced pilot was definitely *not* on the menu. But Saab's engineering ingenuity provided solutions to these and other problems which are to be found in all new prototypes, be they aeroplanes or motor vehicles.

The first flight of the prototype, now designated Saab J21, came- but only just - on 30 July 1943. Test pilot Claes Smith, making another first flight of a Saab prototype, had been instructed to take-off with the flaps lowered to achieve the shortest ground run. Sadly, when the predicted take-off point had been reached and passed and the J21 was still on the ground, Smith found it was too late to abort the take-off. As he thundered through the airfield boundary fence and across a road the aircraft began to lift. He retracted the landing gear and elected to land at a larger airfield. As he did so the wheel-brakes failed, so he popped his anti-spin parachute. Finally, the main landing gear units folded and brought everything to a grinding halt. Crashing through that fence couldn't have done them much good. Later inspection of the aeroplane pointed to the strong possibility of the brakes having been left on during take-off. There was also the chance, of course, that the flaps had been lowered too far. But things got better after that!

Deliveries of the first operational aircraft to the SwAF F8 Wing began in December 1945. Five more Wings had been equipped when production ceased in 1949 with 302 aircraft having been delivered. There were three variants: J21A-1 the base line fighter, J21A-2 an enhanced A-1 and the A21A-3 attack aircraft. They were finally withdrawn from service in July 1954.

Having entered the world of fighters and attack aircraft with an unorthodox design, in 1944 Saab next moved boldly into an entirely different field. It was clear that the end of the Second World War was in sight. Contracts for military aircraft would be few and there would be much unemployment. On the other hand there would be a growing need for new civil transport aircraft and smaller types for private flying. Saab examined both classes of aircraft and at the end of the year work on both began.

In addition to aircraft production the Company considered producing a small motorcar. Plans for this moved ahead very quickly and the first model, Saab 92, was revealed publicly in June 1947 when it was unveiled before members of the Press in Linköping's Staff Club. (Car manufacturer Saab Automobil AB is now jointly owned by Sweden's Investor company and the US General Motors organisation). Saab also went into the boat-building business for a short time in 1947 in its efforts to keep the wolf from the hangar doors. About 250 aluminium rowing boats were produced, numbers of which were exported to some African customers. Another project was a hydrofoil craft but it was not destined to enter production.

With limited knowledge of airline requirements Tord Lidmalm, civil transport project leader, held discussions with ABA Swedish Airlines which was seeking a short-haul twin-engined 30-passenger aircraft. In effect it wanted something which would prove virtually unattainable by numerous aircraft manufacturers: a DC-3 replacement with modern design features but with that venerable aeroplane's low cost of ownership. At the same time, Anders J. Andersson became manager of the Saab 91 light trainer project. Although Swedish, he had been chief designer at Bücker Flugzeugbau in Germany in the 1930s and had designed the renowned series of Jungmann, Jungmeister and Bestmann trainer aircraft for that company. He returned to Sweden in 1939. Work on the transport, now designated Saab 90, began in April 1944 but it was some eight months later that design of the Saab 91 trainer started.

The construction and first flights of both these prototypes was delayed by industrial action by one of the trade unions at the factory. As other work on the Saab 90A-1 progressed the company was stunned by the detailed requirements of the US Civil Aviation Agency for this class of commercial aeroplane. Once again, during the design stages Saab realised that yet another prototype was seriously underpowered. The 1,200 hp Pratt & Whitney R-1830 Twin Wasp radial engines were simply not man enough to provide the performance planned, even though this power unit had been described as 'one of the best all-round radial engines ever built'. Thus, the production aircraft, named the Scandia, had a pair of 1,825 hp R-2180E-1 Twin Wasps developed for the Douglas DC-4 four-engined airliner. But as DC-4 sales slumped this plan was abandoned, so the eighteen Scandias were the only aircraft with this engine. Not the best situation for a new transport.

Meanwhile the little Saab 91 Safir trainer prototype was nearing completion and it first flew on 20 November 1945, powered with a 147 hp de Havilland Gipsy X engine. Small scale production began some five months later, the Swedish and Ethiopian Air Forces buying numbers as trainers and communications aircraft. But it was not until a more powerful 195 hp Lycoming O-435A engine was fitted to produce the Saab 91B that sales 'took-off'. To meet the demand 120 Safirs were built by the Dutch De Schelde company beginning in 1951. Production ceased in 1966 when 323 aircraft had been built. They were exported to twenty-one countries and served with six Air Forces. The Safir was a nice little earner for Saab.

In marked contrast the Scandia was not a success story. Following the prototype's first flight on 16 November 1946, only seventeen more were built for three customers: ABA Swedish Air Lines (later part of the tri-national Scandinavian Airline Systems), Brazil's VASP and Aerovias do Brazil. That said, Saab and the Scandia undoubtedly had a rough ride. Its early engine problems and their rarity, the fact that its cabin was unpressurised and, it must be said, the fact that Saab was a newcomer to the highly competitive civil airliner market, all militated against the Scandia. Finally, Saab had been under the greatest pressure by the Swedish Air Board to ditch the Scandia to provide production capacity for the new J29 jet fighter, which the SwAF desperately needed to fulfill its plan to increase the number of its fighter Wings. The fear that the Korean War could escalate into the Third World War helped to fuel this plan. Ultimately, Saab received compensation from the Board for abandoning Scandia production and handing it over to the Dutch Fokker company, which built only six more aircraft during 1954.

But there was still another ingredient. On 10 March 1947 Saab's first jet aircraft had flown. This was a much-modified J21 twin-boomed fighter powered with a 1,360 kgf (3,000 lb) thrust de Havilland Goblin turbojet. Designated J21R, it was intended to be a low-cost route to gaining jet fighter experience. It proved to be an expensive time-consuming exercise. Initially it was believed that only a small percentage of the airframe would need to be altered. In fact, this was nearer 50 per cent. A total of four prototypes and sixty production examples were built to equip one SwAF fighter Wing, F10, for a year. They were then transferred to two more Wings when, as A21Rs, they were switched to the attack role. In service they won praise as splendid weapons platforms with good take-off and landing characteristics, but their performance didn't measure up to that of contemporary jet fighters.

At this point it is interesting to reflect that during the five year period from July 1943 to September 1948, Saab had flown a new prototype aircraft, each very different from the others, on average every 12 months! Looked at in relation to the Scandia story, one wonders whether the company had been trying to keep too many balls in the air (or get too many different aeroplanes into it) at the same time.

Apart from building cars in its programme to keep its factories busy, in the winter of 1947 Saab made 250 small aluminium boats. They were tested in a school swimming pool because the Stångån river was frozen!

A Saab project which remained as a 'one-off' venture was this hydrofoil craft. Here its designer Kurt Sjögren goes afloat for its first test run.

Unorthodox? That's the Saab J21A. Twin booms, pusher engine, ejection seat; this last piece of kit was fitted after plans to jettison the entire power unit, if the pilot had to get out in an emergency, were abandoned!

The very small frontal area of the J21A, which sat high off the ground, is clearly seen in this photograph taken in 1946.

The J21's pilot sat behind two nose-mounted 13.2 mm and one 20 mm cannon. A 20 mm cannon was also carried in the front end of each tail boom The white-capped muzzle is visible in this view.

View looking forward from under the J21A's tailplane showing the neat installation of the Daimler-Benz DB605 engine and propeller.

Close up of the J21's windscreen and cockpit canopy. Note the bulged canopy and the scalloped rear fairing to improve the rearward view for the pilot.

In the air the J21 had a thrusting appearance as if eager to get on with the job in hand.

No wonder this photograph won the Swedish Press Photographers' Award for The Best Photograph of 1950. It shows an A21A-3 firing four of its eight 14.5 cm underwing rockets.

The first J21R airborne on 6 May 1947. Note the side air intakes for the closely-cowled de Havilland Goblin and high tailplane to be clear of the jet efflux.

The central 'pod' of the J21R housed the armament, pilot and engine. This photograph, taken in April 1948, shows some 'interesting' deformation of the metal skinning on the fins and rudders.

A J21R shows off details of its *al fresco* 1,360 kgf (2,996 lb) thrust de Havilland Goblin engine. New tail booms and fin and rudder assemblies were required to raise the tailplane. This photograph is dated 4 January 1949.

The clean lines of this J21R contributed to its high performance. The muzzles of the 20 mm cannon plus landing lights in the front ends of the tail booms are visible.

The Saab 90 Scandia 25/30-seat regional airliner, was not a howling success. The prototype Saab 90A, SE-BCA, is seen during an early 1947 test flight. Just discernible are the original oval engine cowlings with integral carburettor air intakes.

SE-BCA's engine nacelles were changed to a more orthodox circular form with the carburettor intake below them. Here it flies on a misty day in spring 1947.

Uniquely Saab. The external shape of Saab's first motorcar, the Saab 92 which first appeared in 1947, clearly owed much to the Company's knowledge of aerodynamics. This design philosophy characterised Saab cars for the next thirty years.

The sixth Scania SS-BSB was the first of eight delivered to the newly formed Scandinavian Airlines System. Named *Gardar Viking*, it was subsequently sold to VASP in Brazil.

Saab chief test pilot Claes Smith peers out of the Second Officer's window of a Scandia in May 1947

Pictured in 1949, the first Scandia on show with a Saab 91B Safir.

The first Scandia in VASP livery before it was sold as a private executive aircraft.

PP-SQR was one of six new Scandias delivered to VASP, which eventually bought from other airlines all but one of the eighteen Scandias built. It then operated them until the mid-1960s. This aircraft continued in service until July 1969.

Scene in 1953. One man directs the traffic, another watches a Lansen prototype and ignores SAS's Scandia taxiing behind him. The little Saab 210 on the right waits to see what will happen next.

The unpainted and unregistered prototype Saab 91, seen in November 1945, with its de Havilland Gipsy Major X engine and wooden propeller. Beside it is a fine example of Saab's automotive design and engineering skills.

The first production Saab 91A Safir tourer/trainer SE-AUN, seen mounted on floats in 1946. With 147 hp de Havilland Gipsy Major X engines, forty-eight Safir 91As were built, many for the SwAF and the Imperial Ethiopian Air Force.

The pilot of SE-AUN leans nonchalantly from its cabin. Much of the design and structural details of this little aeroplane are clearly visible.

Small scale production of Saab 91A Safirs. Pictured on 20 November 1946, are eight aircraft in various stages of construction. Two have their de Havilland Gipsy Major X engines and wooden propellers fitted.

Very mini-airliner? This Safir B, registered D-EBAB, was owned by Lufthansa. Its 195 hp Lycoming flat six cylinder engine upped its performance over the Gipsy-engined Safir A version.

Dual control cockpit of the Safir B. The 'standard six' panel is on the left, with engine instrumentation in the centre and radio controls on the right.

Is this 'wooden wonder' a Safir landing gear test rig or a ground trainer? It has weight boxes, rudder bar possibly operating brakes and a towing bridle. Or it could be for a carnival procession? Answers on a postcard please.

A large access door has been removed from this Safir's wing to reveal - a machine gun and ammunition box?

During the early 1950s the De Schelde company in Holland built 120 Safir Bs and Cs. This Safir C, with all four seats occupied, shows the partly retracted nosewheel, a feature of all Safirs.

Five of a large number of Safir Ds with 180 hp Lycoming engines, which were operated by Holland's Rijksluchtvaartschool - Airline Pilots' School - fly in formation.

In 1956 the Finnish Air Force ordered twenty Safir Ds. The first of three float-mounted de Havilland Canada DHC-2 Beavers operated by the Finnish Air Force can be seen in the background.

Swedish Air Force Safir Bs built by De Schelde lined up for a day's flying. Two pupil pilots with seat-type parachutes prepare for an aerial lesson.

42

Four

Enter the Serious Jets

'The first Western European jet fighter to have swept wings, an all-moving tailplane, automatic leading edge slats and full-span ailerons/flaps'. This fulsome description applies to the Saab 29. But it was not its 25 degree swept wing which drew most attention. It was its tubby fuselage, with the pilot mounted on top and the tail unit sticking out behind, which was responsible for its nickname 'Tunnan', which means barrel. Now, let's look at its history.

Born in 1945 as the JxR project, it was redesignated R1001 in the following year. There followed an intensive two years designing and building of the first prototype, styled the Saab 29, employing the most technologically advanced processes and equipment which led to its first flight on 1 September 1948 by Sqn Ldr Bob Moore, who had been appointed chief test pilot. Once again, there was a perplexing problem which marred this prototype's first venture into the air. Moore found that the aircraft's acceleration was slow and that he couldn't reach the planned speed for the flight. The cause was soon discovered when the pilot of the accompanying 'chase' aircraft noticed that the landing gear doors, which should have closed when the gear was retracted, were still open. Back on the ground Saab engineers soon set matters right - no doubt much to the relief of project leader Lars Brising.

While large sections of the Saab organisation were busy with this latest fighter, the project designers were looking closely at the perceived threat from any future hostile air attack on Sweden. This was envisaged as single high-flying jet bombers; thus their thoughts revolved around a fast climbing, heavily armed and electronically-equipped fighter aeroplane. Because Saab's production of aviation equipment of various kinds was growing, a new factory was taken over at Jönköping in 1950. In that year Tryggve Holm, a mining engineer by profession, became Saab's managing director. He was to oversee many changes in the aviation industry and lead the Company with distinction and success for some seventeen years. There was also a change of product line at Trollhättan, where the factory was now devoted to Saab motorcar production. Initially, it had been slow - only four cars a day; but things got better after that too. Now back to the J29 Tunnan.

In May 1951, F13 at Norrköping became the first SwAF Wing to take delivery of its J29As. The J29B had increased fuel capacity for longer range while the A-29B equipped two SwAF Attack Wings. An unarmed photo-reconnaissance variant, packed with cameras and other equipment, was designated the S29C. A standard J29B set a new 500 km closed circuit record of 982 kph (607 mph) and a pair of S29C s broke the 1,000 km closed circuit record averaging 900 kph (560 mph).

In October 1961 five SwAF J29Bs flew to the Congo as part of a United Nations force and took part in offensive operations against opposing Katangan forces. In the following year two

S29C reconnaissance aircraft and four more J29Bs joined them. Four aircraft returned home, two crashed, one was damaged beyond repair and the rest were blown up.

One prototype and numbers of J29Bs were subsequently modified with a new wing having a broader chord outboard section and were redesignated J29E. Although the first four variants were powered by the 2,270 kgf (5,000 lb) thrust de Havilland Ghost turbojet engine, which gave them a top speed of some 1,030 kph (640 mph), pilots were not entirely satisfied with the 2,438 m (8,000 ft) per minute climb rate. The quickest remedy was an afterburner system for this engine. Britain's de Havilland Engine Company had not yet come up with such a system for the Ghost, so Svenska Flygmotor designed a very effective one which increased the Ghost's thrust to some 2,800 kgf (6,100 lb) and the aircraft's climb rate to over 3,350 m (11,000 ft) per minute. The service ceiling, top speed and take-off performance were also improved. With this installation and the new wing the fighter was designated J29F; it was much liked by the squadron pilots who flew it. The type was withdrawn from first line service in 1967 but a number, which were converted for target towing and for training purposes, remained in service for about ten more years. A grand total of 661 J29 'Flying Barrels' were rolled out, still the company's biggest production programme.

Although Saab had had great hopes of selling the 'Tunnan' to other countries, the Austrian Air Force - Österreichische Heerefliegerkräfte, one of the world's oldest having been formed in 1892 - was the only one to have it. In 1961 a total of thirty ex-SwAF J29Fs were delivered to Austria and remained in service for eleven years.

Recognised as a neutral European country, the Swedish Government always made clear that its Armed Forces were for the defence of its neutrality. To be effective they had to keep pace with technological developments in other countries. This was particularly important for the air defence system. As early as 1946 the Air Board and the SwAF were looking a decade ahead in formulating the type of fighter aircraft which would be required to secure Sweden's borders. The results of their studies, led by Arthur Bråsjö, produced the Saab project 1150 which, at the end of 1948, was given the nod for further development. It materialised as a conventional single-engined swept wing two-seater aeroplane able to operate in the attack, reconnaissance and all-weather fighting roles. Three aircraft for the price of one? Well, not quite.

It was extensively - and expensively - equipped with radar, a sophisticated fire-control system and heavy armament. It moved Saab design engineers into the electronic age. In addition, the Saab 32, as it was designated, was designed using entirely new techniques. And it looked right! There was one fairly major hiccup, however. Both of the two first-choice engines for Saab 32, now named Lansen, were cancelled. Instead a 3,400 kgf (7,500 lb) thrust Rolls-Royce Avon turbojet was used to power the first prototype. After the first flight on 3 November 1952, test pilot Bengt Olow commented 'The 'Thirty Two' appears to be promising in all respects. It will become a favourite with pilots'. But before that could become fact the aircraft had to be built in quantity, so the production facilities at Linköping were expanded to cope with this work.

One of the five prototypes provided Saab with an historic aviation milestone when it exceeded Mach 1.0 during a test flight. It was going downhill at the time, of course, but was reported to have been 'under complete control'!

Three basic production variants were built. The A32A Lansen attack aircraft, a photo-reconnaissance version designated S32C and the J32B all-weather fighter. All were powered by more advanced Rolls-Royce Avons than those in the prototypes which were licence-built by Svenska Flygmotor. With Swedish-developed afterburners the thrust nudged 6,660 kgf (14,700 lb). A small batch of J32Bs were converted for target towing and other training roles.

The first deliveries of A32As to the SwAF were made in December 1955 and within two years all four Attack Wings had been re-equipped. A32Cs and J32Bs both entered service in 1959, the all-weather fighters equipping four Wings while one Wing operated the reconnaisance variant. Two final variants, the J32D and 'E were produced by converting J32Bs for target towing and training roles. Production of the highly effective Lansen ceased in April 1960 when 456 had been built.

One of the prototype Saab J29s photographed nearing completion on 1 June 1948. Note the air intake's high-density wood leading edge ring and the 'clear view' cockpit canopy.

The narrow track main landing gear and unusual mid-wing configuration are interesting design features of this unpainted J29 prototype seen in 1948.

No wonder Lars Brising, the J29's project manager, dubbed this aeroplane the 'Tunnan' (Barrel). But the tubby appearance of this second prototype seen on 18 February 1949, belied its high performance and good handling characteristics.

Like gasping goldfish fifteen J29 fuselages are stacked in the factory ready to have their engines, landing gear and 11 m (36 ft) span one-piece wings fitted.

Successfully Saab. By the end of 1950, 1,248 Saab 92s like this 1950 model, which had had only minor modifications, had been produced.

With two JATO - Jet Assisted Take-Off - bottles at full squirt plus its de Havilland Ghost turbojet's 2,270 kgf (5,000 lb) thrust, a missile-laden A29B attack aircraft tucks up its landing gear and rapidly gets airborne.

Rows of J29s and an array of staging and steps typified this 1951 scene during this aircraft's production era at Linköping.

Photographed in 1952, a pilot with a back-type parachute climbs aboard an armed J29. Four 20 mm cannon were mounted under the nose air intake. A couple of landing lights are also there.

A J29 in its natural environment as it flies high in the sunshine over Sweden in 1953.

A quartet of S29C unarmed photo-reconnaissance aircraft patrol the sky in impeccable stepped-up echelon formation.

A pair of J29Fs, with new 'saw tooth' increased chord outer wings, bank steeply away from the photographic aeroplane. Each carries twenty-four underwing rocket projectiles.

Royal Lance: prototype A32 Lansen, pictured in 1953, with original flush air intakes but production standard boundary layer wing fences. King Gustaf Adolf VI's signature is on the nose by the letter 'U'.

The old aviation saying 'If it looks right, it *is* right' nearly applied to the Lansen. Pre-first flight trials and subsequent air testing proved that some changes to the shapes of the flush air intakes and fuselage were necessary.

A J32 Lansen readied for a test flight. Compare the air intake shape with those of the aircraft in the two previous photographs.

An A32A attack Lansen on show. Beneath it is the formidable array of external weapons which could be carried in addition to the Lansen's four nose-mounted 20 mm cannon.

A32A Lansen attack aircraft of the Swedish Air Force's 6 Wing. All appear to have patchy paintwork on their fuselage flanks. Something similar can be seen on the wing surface of the nearest aircraft.

One of two J32B prototypes gets airborne for a test flight.

Ooh-La-La Lansen. A J32B Lansen at a Paris Salon Aeronautique at Le Bourget Airport. A Saab J35 Draken's fin tip and nose can be seen behind it.

The extremely fine finish on the external skin surfaces of the Paris Show Lansen can be seen in this close up photograph of the revised air intake.

Saab's lean, mean, night machine. One of the 120 J32B all-weather and night fighter Lansens, this one belonged to the Swedish Air Force's 12 Wing, the first to receive them in mid-1958.

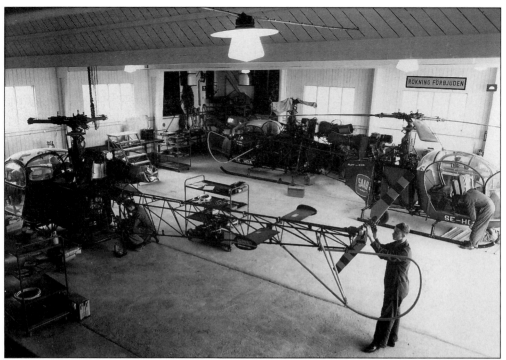

In 1958 Saab negotiated an agreement with Sud-Aviation to build and sell the Alouette II helicopter. The first one was test flown in May of 1959. Here, two of these general purpose helicopters are being assembled at Norrköping.

This photograph's caption issued by Sweden's FFV Aerotech reads 'The Swedish Air Force J32B Lansen with the FFV Aerotech GAMMA-POD collecting GAMMA emitting radionuclides in the tropopause'. So now you know!

Front fuselages of S32C reconnaissance Lansen's being produced.

Two of Saab's development Lansens. The nearer aircraft appears to have a Viggen's nose cone for aerodynamic flight testing. Behind it is a Lansen used for Saab's ejector seat trials.

Five

The Delta Dynasty plus One

The thoughts of Saab project engineers in the late 1940s on the best defence against attack by high flying bombers soon crystallised around an all-weather interceptor with a double-delta wing, a shape developed exclusively by Saab, and a Mach 1.5 capability, plus many other qualities. Saab was breaking new ground with a vengeance, for it had virtually no experience or expertise in the field of supersonic aerodynamics or manned flight.

The best way to obtain these was to build a model and fly it - which Saab did. But this 'model', the Saab 210 or 'Mini-Draken', had a 7 m (23 ft) wing span, was powered by an 499 kgf (1,100 lb) thrust Armstrong Siddeley Adder turbojet, had a top speed of 565 kph (350 mph) and required a human-sized pilot to fly it! He was Bengt Olow, who first put daylight under its little landing gear wheels on 21 January 1952. Though small, this experimental aeroplane provided answers to many of the design and aerodynamic questions being asked by project leader Erik Bratt and his team, plus experience of jet flight generally with a delta-winged aeroplane. Nearly 900 flights were made. Meanwhile, design of the full scale Saab 35 Draken was pressed ahead and the first flight of this single-seat interceptor fighter prototype took place on 25 October 1955. It is recorded that, although its engine did not have an afterburner, this prototype 'accidentally' went supersonic while climbing during this flight!

The original plan to make this an all-Swedish aeroplane was shelved when development of the STAL Glan turbojet engine was cancelled. Instead, the five prototypes had RM 5 Swedish-built 3,628 kgf (8,000 lb) thrust Rolls-Royce Avon 100 engines, but 5,000 kgf (11,000 lb) thrust Avon Series 200s, licence-built by Svenska Flygmotor as the RM 6B, powered the production Drakens. With the addition of the Swedish afterburning system the thrust topped 6,500 kgf (14,300 lb). An interesting feature of later Drakens was the twin-tailwheel installation which enabled a very nose-high landing attitude to be used, without causing damage to the fuselage tail-end, for aerodynamic braking from the large area double-delta wing. This shortened the landing run and minimised wheel braking - an important feature on snow-covered strips.

J35A Drakens entered SwAF service late in 1959 with F13 Wing at Norrköping, which flew these aircraft to the corners of their flight envelope, reaching the required Mach 1.8 maximum speed. Eight more Draken sub-types were produced: the J35B with advanced electronic equipment and able to carry a range of external armament and tanks; a two-seat trainer designated Sk-35C in SwAF service; the J35D powered by the Rolls-Royce Avon 300 producing 12,787 kgf (17,637 lb) thrust with afterburner; a photo reconnaissance aircraft, widely used by the SwAF with the designation S35E to replace the Lansen; the J35F, an improved 'D with uprated electronics and armament. During the late 1980s some seventy-five 'Fs were updated and given greater range to become J35Js. In 1968 Denmark ordered the first of some fifty Drakens for the attack, reconnaissance and training roles in the Danish Air Force - *Kongelige Dansk Flyvevåbnet*. Two years later Valmet OY began assembly of Saab 35XS Drakens for the Finnish Air Force - *Ilmavoimat* - which received about forty-five for similar roles. Austria took delivery of twenty-four ex-SwAF J35Ds. Overall Draken production totalled 612 aircraft.

The huge development programmes which, over the years, had brought to operational status the Draken and its predecessors on the Saab production lines, had created the need for a wide range of new equipment: radars, fire control and bombing systems including a unique 'toss-bomb' sight, auto pilot systems, ejector seats, navigational aids, guided missiles, space satellite work - the list goes on. There was, too, Saab's licenced-assembly of French Alouette II helicopters at Norrköping plus the marketing of Morane Saulnier Rallye light aircraft and Hughes helicopters in Scandinavia and hovercraft development. It was in 1965 that the Saab Board decided to rename the Company to more accurately reflect the fact that it was no longer simply an aeroplane builder. For this reason the Company became restyled SAAB Aktiebolaget.

While production of the Draken was under way, Saab designers were working on plans for something quite different. Originally this company-funded aeroplane was to have been a delta-winged executive jet transport for businessmen to wing their way around Europe. It was to be a sort of twin-jet successor to the Safir. Sadly, the Euro-businessmen were not interested, even though the design, the Saab 105, materialised as a more conventional high-wing monoplane. But when the door marked 'Air Taxi' remained closed, another marked 'Military Trainer' swung wide open. The SwAF had come to the rescue for it badly needed a new 'all-through' jet trainer to replace the ageing de Havilland Vampire. The first prototype was first flown by Karl-Erik Fernberg on 1 July 1963 and the two-seater side-by-side Type 105 entered SwAF service as the Sk60 in April 1966.

One small blush-making event occurred at the 1972 SBAC Farnborough Display where the Saab 105 was making its first appearance. 'Its pilot had the misfortune to cross that celebrated dividing line between pilots who have landed with the wheels up and those who are going to' said John Blake, the renowned commentator! This had no ill effects on the type for production totalled 150 in three principal sub-types: the Sk60A trainer, 'B attack aircraft and 'C attack/reconnaissance aeroplane. At least one Sk60D was converted to a four-seater to give training in civil airline communications procedures. An export version, the Saab 105XT, with more powerful 1,293 kgf (2,850 lb) General Electric J-85-17B engines first flew in 1967 and formed the basis for forty aircraft delivered to the Austrian Air Force as the Saab 105OE.

Readers of this Saab saga will not fail to note that the SwAF operational planners and the Company's project designers began their studies for new types of aircraft very many years ahead of the date on which they entered service. Using their experience, careful interpretation of Intelligence reports and reading the signs and signals coming from the aviation and defence world, they produced their shopping list of requirements for an 'ideal' aeroplane for service some ten or even twenty years into the future.

While the Saab company had had several big production programmes before 1960, they were all overshadowed by an aeroplane which began life as Aircraft System 37 but was later named Viggen - which means Thunderbolt. First thoughts on this outstanding military aeroplane began in about 1952-53. Some eight years later the Swedish Air Board wrote their specification for a multi-role aircraft around a Saab proposal. For a fighter it was big in every sense. Over 5.6

m (18 ft) tall and nearly 16.5 m (54 ft) long, the heaviest version weighed in at some 18,000 kg (35,600 lb). It was designed for a top speed of Mach 2.0 and with the ability to clamber up to 18,000 m (59,000 ft) courtesy of the 12,750 kgf (28,000 lb) thrust from its single licence-built Pratt & Whitney JT8D-22/7300 turbofan engine with its Swedish afterburner. (Well, apart from production figures, that's got all the numbers out of the way.) Its most unusual feature, however, was its flapped delta foreplane to provide control in pitch and to generate lift in combination with the delta wing. This aerodynamic configuration (original thinking included a blown foreplane, but this was abandoned) was conceived and developed by Saab to give the Viggen great agility in the air and its amazing STOL capability which enables it to operate from any 460 m (1,500 ft) straight stretch of roadway. In a country with very few and widely scattered air bases this 'runway-multiplier' concept greatly enhances Sweden's air defence system. In addition, the Viggen was designed to be turned around between operational flights by five National Servicemen in ten minutes.

The first of seven Viggen prototypes got airborne on 8 February 1967 in the hands of Eric Dahlström. The following spring an order for 180 aircraft was received by Saab and the first production Viggens, AJ37 attack aircraft to succeed the Lansen, were delivered in 1971. (The second prototype, 37002, appeared in the 1972 Farnborough Display where the Viggen became a long-standing favourite.) There followed, first, the Sk37 two-seat trainer, the SF37 photo-reconnaissance aircraft, then the maritime reconnaissance SH37 with deliveries of the JA37 all-weather interceptor coming in 1979. A total of 329 Viggens were built, many still equipping SwAF squadrons with plans for them to continue until sometime around 2012.

While the Viggen programme was getting off the ground, it was announced in December 1968 that Saab was to merge with Scania-Vabis, a large Swedish commercial vehicle manufacturer which, like Saab, belonged to the Skandinaviska Enskilda Banken Group. The aim was to make more effective use of their joint resources for research, development, manufacturing and marketing. Thereafter the company was named Saab-Scania Aktiebolag.

Saab 210 in the snow. This 'pocket project', Sweden's first delta-winged aircraft, was a flying test bed built to provide Saab designers and pilots with information on performance and handling characteristics of this wing shape.

The Saab 210 gets airborne for an early test flight. Nearly 900 flights were made during its flight research programme.

Because of limited internal volume the Saab 210's landing gear was only partially retractable. Here chief test pilot Bengt Olow positions his little aeroplane to show the double-delta wing planform.

Though small, the Saab 210 had room for modern features like an ejector seat and retractable landing gear. Here it pops a braking parachute to reduce the landing run.

The first prototype Saab 35 Draken with a 'barber's pole' striped pitot boom. The vertical mast on top of the fin belongs to a distant ground installation, not the aeroplane.

Four Draken prototypes. The third aircraft has an additional window aft of the cockpit canopy, but apart from a paint job, externally they all look alike.

The pilot keeps a wary eye on the photographer as he hauls this missile-carrying J35A Draken off a roadway and tucks up its landing gear.

In 1972 Finland leased six of these J35B Drakens from the Swedish Air Force for training in readiness for the delivery of their new Saab 35XS Drakens four years later.

About twenty-five of these Sk35C Draken two-seat trainers were produced for the Swedish Air Force.

The Austrian Air Force bought twenty-four 'somewhat used J35D Drakens' (to use Saab's description of these aircraft). Here are eight of them.

Specially-designed mini-cameras were produced to fit into the small nose of the S35E Draken reconnaissance aircraft. This one is all tanked up ready for a long ranging 'recce' mission...

... and here is another one in the air.

Emphasising Swedish defence forces' flexibility, this J35F all-weather interceptor/attack aircraft operates from a roadway during an air exercise.

The pilot of a SwAF 1 Wing J35F talks to a member of the ground crew during an air exercise while his aircraft is prepared for another sortie.

Some Draken pilots, like the one in this 13 Wing Draken, used a braking parachute after touch down...

... while others didn't, like this chap, peering over the nose of his 4 Wing Draken, who's relying on aerodynamic and wheel braking to stop him before he runs out of runway.

Major sub-assembly line, seen in about 1971, showing the Draken in full production.

A misty Swedish roadway, more used to vehicles and braking systems of a different kind, doubles as a landing strip for a SwAF J35F Draken using a braking parachute at touch down.

Twin tailwheels, touching down first, enable this SwAF pilot to raise his J35F Draken's nose high when landing without damaging its tail end on the ground.

Three of the fifty-one Drakens sold to the Danish Air Force between 1968 and 1976.

'Mm. Looks a nice day for a bit of aviating'. This SwAF 10 Wing pilot scans the sky before a flight. Some sixty J35Fs equipped with updated avionics, more internal fuel and greater missile punch, became J35J Drakens - like this one.

The seventh production Saab 105, designated Sk60A, belonged to the Swedish Air Force's F5 Flying School. This variant was powered by two 743 kgf (1,640 lb) thrust Turbomeca Aubisque turbofan engines.

This civil-registered Saab 105XT with 1,293 kgf (2,850 lb) thrust General Electric engines, became an export development aircraft and was used for many years to test fly a range of underwing stores.

The official caption describes this aeroplane as a Saab 105G. It is the export development Saab 105XT aircraft with a more military 'uniform' and serial.

Armed Spies. SwAF Sk60Cs taxi out on an air exercise. Configured for combined reconnaissance and attack roles, they carry nose-mounted 180 degree panoramic cameras and 13.5 mm rocket projectiles.

Two underwing 30 mm cannon pods give this camera-equipped Sk60C reconnaissance aircraft a hefty punch. Note the rocket projectiles on ground trolleys.

An Sk60C carries a pair of test Rb05 guided missiles developed by Saab.

Saab's export development aircraft, with a variety of antennae, carries a brace of 30 mm cannon pods and two Sidewinder air-to-air missiles.

'See amid the winter's snow'. The Saab 105XT is seen with an experimental target-towing installation.

Close up of the target-towing equipment. Inboard is the winch pod powered by a variable pitch ram air turbine with a towed target on the outboard pylon. Note General Electric's logo on the engine nacelle.

SE-XBZ flies with an FFV Red Baron reconnaissance pod under its port wing.

The first of forty Saab 105OEs ordered for the Austrian Air Force in 1968. This export version, based on the 105XT, could carry a 2,000 kg (4,410 lb) external load, nearly three times that of the standard Sk60Bs.

In addition to their much improved load-carrying capability, these Austrian Air Force Saab 105XT's top speed increased by 205 kph (128 mph) and range by 980 km (609 miles) over those of the Sk60Bs.

Hidden in the smoke from the 13.5 cm rockets it has just fired is a Saab 105XT. The camera has 'frozen' six missiles in flight.

This full scale mock up of the Saab 37 Viggen multi-role aircraft was revealed publicly for the first time in April 1965...

... and this was the real thing. Note the 'clean' wing, which lacks the later stores pylons and fairings, and the rear fuselage's straight top line. The small fin-tip pod and foreplane flaps are interesting features.

The still unpainted first Viggen with Swedish Air Force markings. The fin-tip pod has disappeared and the short nose-mounted pitot boom has been replaced with a much longer one.

Eric Dahlström, Saab chief test pilot, who made the first flight with the Viggen on 8 February 1967.

The Viggen's hot end. The world's first aircraft to have its thrust reverser built into the airframe, it was a bit 'naughty' at first, but Saab engineers soon solved the problems.

Production AJ37 Viggen attack aircraft showing the fuselage's dorsal hump, introduced to cure some instability when external stores were being carried.

The pilot of the second prototype Viggen banks his aircraft to show the two underwing Rb04 sea-skimming anti-ship guided missiles.

This 1973 photograph shows a Swedish Air Force Sk37 two-seat trainer with a ventral drop tank. Sk37s were flown by F 15 Wing's conversion training unit.

An AJ37 Viggen armed with five rocket pods banks steeply away from the photographic aircraft.

With reheat wicks turned to full bore, AJ37 Viggens 37052 and '55 split seconds after becoming airborne in a cloud of steam and spray from Farnborough's wet runway during the 1974 Society of British Aerospace Companies' Display.

In more tranquil mood, a pair of Swedish Air Force F15 Wing Viggens patrol the Swedish coast.

Superchargingly Saab. The Saab 99 Turbo was given its first public showing in 1977 at the Frankfurt Motor Show.

Model of the Saab B3LA light attack/trainer aircraft project of 1976. It was rejected by the Swedish Government due to lack of funds in February 1979.

'Don't point them at me - they may go off'. The pilot of this AJ37 Viggen draws a bead on the photographer during systems efficiency tests with a pair of Rb04E anti-ship missiles in August 1983.

An AJ37 Viggen taxies from a 'hide' deep in a snow-covered forest while another one waits to move onto the forest roadway during an exercise.

Viggen Centurion. On 20 August 1985, the 100th Viggen, a JA37, was handed over to Swedish Air Force Commander Lt General Sven-Olof Olson by Harald Schröder, who had headed the System 37 Industrial Delegation.

One of six Saab JA37 Viggen prototypes, of which at least four were reported to be converted AJ37s. Note the air intake shape, long pitot boom and nose leg configuration.

'There's a moose on the loose...' A Saab car undergoes a crash test simulating being hit by a passing moose! Aircraft only have bird strikes to worry about. And missiles, of course.

An SF37 Viggen carrying podded night reconnaissance systems, centreline ventral fuel tank and electronic countermeasures pod.

A pair of JA37 Viggens armed with two underwing British Aerospace Skyflash missiles and two Sidewinder missiles below the fuselage.

On 29 June 1990, the last JA37 Viggen was delivered to the Swedish Air Force. Saab Programme Manager Sune Andersson was there to watch test pilot Lars Ruderström fly it away.

A JA37 Viggen all-weather fighter/strike aircraft with updated avionics, a 12,750 kgf (28,000 lb) thrust RM8B engine (Volvo Flygmotor-built and developed Pratt & Whitney JT8D).

Six

Seats for One, Two, Thirty-Five or Fifty

Designed by MFI - Malmö Flygindustri AB, *not* the furniture people - Saab added the MFI-15 light trainer and observation aircraft to its products range when it bought the company in March 1968. The first one flew on 11 July 1969. Although the SwAF chose the Scottish Aviation Bulldog as its new primary trainer, Saab developed the aircraft into the more powerful MFI-17 close support aeroplane. Able to carry underwing stores and named, not surprisingly, the Supporter, it flew in 1972. Supporters have been supplied to the Air Forces of Pakistan, Denmark, Norway and to the Danish Army. Production is about 300 including more than 100 assembled and licence-built as the Mushtaq in Pakistan.

Casting our minds back some thirty-five years to the Scandia airliner, one of the reasons for its failure was lack of a pressurised cabin. During the mid-1970s Saab-Scania decided to move into the commercial aircraft field to balance its heavy commitment to military aeroplanes. There followed about five years study of 'paper projects', during which it realised that it needed a partner company to share the huge costs of developing an airliner from scratch and to provide the marketing 'know-how' which it lacked. As the major market appeared to be in the USA the Swedish company began discussions with Fairchild Industries, which had the required knowledge and experience there. On 25 January 1980, the two companies signed an agreement to create a new 35-seat regional turboprop aircraft, with a pressurised cabin of sufficient height to enable passengers to stand up! Development and production was shared between the two companies and the first SF340 was rolled out at Linköping on 25 January 1983, before King Carl Gustaf XVI, who signed his name on the prototype's shiny white nose. The first aircraft went into airline service with launch customer Crossair of Switzerland in mid-June 1984. During the next two years Saab-Scania took complete control of the SF340 programme and moved all production to Sweden. When Fairchild withdrew from the partnership, the aeroplane became the Saab 340. The Company's balancing act now made the scales slightly loaded towards commercial aeroplanes. It had achieved this by producing an airliner embodying advanced technologies, offering operational economies and doing it at the right time. By January 1996, 380 aircraft had been delivered to operators on five continents; during mid-1997 the 450th aircraft was on the production line. That's a success story! Just two other things: the Saab 340B, which flies as an Airborne Early Warning and Control aircraft carrying on its back the long antennae for Ericsson's Erieye Mission System which is based on new generation active phased-array radar technology, and the Saab340-200 SAR high performance maritime patrol derivative, are also in production.

On the other side of the scales, Saab Military Aircraft was beavering away at a replacement for the Viggen in all of its roles, but half its weight, with the same performance and 30 per cent cheaper! No mean task. But Saab has never shied away from being innovative in its aim of leading the field. The Swedish Government made clear that industry must share design and development costs. A consortium - IG JAS - was formed by Saab-Scania, Volvo Flygmotor, Ericsson Radio Systems and FFV Maintenance to create the new aircraft, the JAS 39 Gripen. (JAS - Jakt/Attack/Spaning - fighter/attack/reconnaissance)

A lightweight multi-role aircraft, it combines these three roles in one airframe and has been described as 'the pioneer of a completely new generation of combat aircraft'. The pilot can reconfigure the Gripen's systems' functions to give it the characteristics required for different missions while a secure data link allows him to transfer information from his systems and sensors to other Gripens in flight. Amazing! Using the well proven foreplane and delta wing configuration with a fly-by-wire system, the Gripen's close-combat agility surpasses that of the Viggen. Its maximum speed is Mach 1.8 and it inherits the Viggen's exceptional STOL characteristics.

The consortium got Government go-ahead for the Gripen in May 1982. The prototype was rolled-out on 26 April 1987 and first flew on 9 December 1988. Deliveries to the SwAF F7 Wing at Såtenäs began during the early autumn 1994. The two-seat JAS39B first flew on 29 April 1996. If deliveries go to plan, 210 Gripens will be equipping 12 SwAF squadrons by 2006.

A new generation of commercial aeroplanes had also arrived with the Saab 2000 jet-prop airliner. Regional airlines wanted an aircraft with jet speed performance for passenger appeal, shorter flight times and the ability to slot into the pure jet aircraft stream arriving and departing at international airports. However they also wanted it to have the operating economies and environmental friendliness of the turboprop! The Saab 2000 is a propeller-driven jet which flies faster, higher and more quietly than any of its forebears, and does it more cost-effectively than any of its pure-jet contemporaries.

A 50/58-seat regional aeroplane, the Saab 2000, makes wide use of metal-to-metal bonding and composite materials. It is powered by two 6,000 shp Allison AE2100 engines driving Dowty six swept composite-bladed propellers. This combination provides the urge to produce a cruising speed of 685 kph (426 mph). Inside the cabin, which is furnished to a very high standard of comfort, an active sound control system keeps noise levels to a minimum.

Roll-out of the first aeroplane was on 14 December 1991 when Queen Silvia of Sweden autographed its pristine fuselage. The Saab 2000 entered service in 1994, with Switzerland's Crossair again being the launch customer, and is already making its mark in airline circles where, as these words are being written, over forty are in service on three continents. An unusual fact about the Saab 2000's 24.6 m (81 ft) span wing is that it is built in one piece tip-to-tip. No matter how far the rest of the aircraft travels in its lifetime, its wing will have clocked up some 3,750 km (2,330 miles) more! How so? The wing is produced by the CASA company in Spain and is delivered from Seville to Linköping by road on specially designed 28 m (92 ft) long vehicles.

Today the Saab Group is a significant part of Sweden's engineering industry. With more than sixty years experience in aviation, Saab Aircraft and Saab Military Aircraft have scaled the heights of innovative design and production of aeroplanes for many differing roles. Saab Aircraft Finance Group is a leasing company for the Saab 340 and 2000 regional airliners; Saab Dynamics produces guided weapons and a range of electronic systems and equipment; Saab Training Systems manufactures simulators and military training systems; Saab Combitech works in the information technology, space, and electronics fields; Saab Helikopter is a distributor of helicopters in Nordic countries.

Now wholly owned by the investment company Investor, Saab faces the challenge of the New Millenium. It is armed with a long-term industrial strategy allied to a work force of nearly 8,000 skilled employees plus a range of well established products and innovative advanced projects. This is Saab in 1997, its 60th Anniversary year.

When Saab bought MFI in March 1968, work on the MFI-15 Safari', intended as a light trainer for the Swedish Air Force and Army, was in hand. Although it could operate as a 'tail-dragger' on wheels it could also use skis. It didn't win the trainer contract, but Saab rarely gives up hope.

Powered by a 200 hp Lycoming flat four-cylinder engine, the MFI-17 Supporter multi-purpose light aircraft was developed from the MFI-15. Underwing strong points carried external stores or armament.

With a tricycle landing gear the MFI-17 Supporter has been used for supply-dropping missions. This one is seen in Ethiopia engaged on famine relief operations.

A Supporter releases eight assorted packs during supply-dropping trials.

Rocket pods could be carried by the Supporter when operating in close support of ground forces.

A Danish Air Force T-17 Supporter light trainer/Army cooperation aircraft.

New Saab-Scania aircraft factory and office buildings at Linköping in June 1982.

Model of the Saab Transporter, one of the stages of project design of the mid-1970s which was to lead to the SF340.

94

Because of the large crowd of 'goofers', they may be watching the mating of the first SF340 fuselage and wings. Three other aircraft are being built at the far end of the shop.

Already carrying the Crossair livery, the first prototype SF340, SE-ISF, stands ready for the royal roll-out on 27 October 1982, before King Carl Gustaf XVI.

Under flags of Sweden and the USA, a large gathering of the two countries' aviation top brass witnessed the roll-out. King Carl Gustaf XVI is seated in the centre.

Saab pulled out all the stops - and the first SF340 - at the ceremony. The aircraft carried launch customer Crossair's markings on one side and Air Midwest's on the other.

The SF340 first flew on 25 January 1983. The landing gear was not retracted for this flight and followed the prudent pattern set by Claes Smith's first flight in the Saab 17 in May 1940!

Three days and several flights later, SE-ISF's landing gear was retracted for the first time. Of more importance perhaps, it was also lowered for the landing.

A triumphant Saab group after the SF340's first flight. From left to right: Rolf Ljungkvist, Director-Civil Aircraft Sector; Olle Espina, Technical Director-SF340 airliner; Tore Gullstrand, President-Aerospace Division; Per Pellebergs, Saab-Scania Chief Test Pilot; Eric Sjöberg, Project Test Pilot; John Wright, Technical Director SF340 programme.

The second SF340, SE-ISA, in Saab house colours was rolled out on 28 March 1982.

Saab-Scania and Fairchild Industries demonstrated the first two SF340 regional airliners to be built at the Paris Air Show from May 26 to June 5 1983.

Scandinavian Airlines System's SF340 Training Centre was opened on 14 February 1984. From left to right in front of the flight simulator: Eric Wahren, SAS Manager SF340 Training Centre; Tom Turner, President and CEO Saab Fairchild Joint Venture; Kurt Ahlborg, Vice President-support SF340; Birgitta Rydbeck, Director SAS Flight Academy.

'*Viva El Tres Cientos Quarente!*' During three weeks in early 1984, the second and third aircraft logged some 113 hours on demonstration flights from Spain's Granada airport.

As part of the SF340 test and development programme, during February 1984 the first prototype was fitted with winglets to assess any improvement in drag characteristics.

Moritz Suter, Crossair's president on the right, receives the delivery documents for his first SF340, HB-AHA, from Tomy Hjort of Saab-Scania aircraft division on 6 June 1984.

Crossair's first SF340 gets smartly airborne from Linköping for its delivery flight to Basle, Switzerland, after Mortiz Suter had received the documentation.

On 12 June 1984, Pope John Paul II flew into Lugano Airport in Crossair's new SF340. He is seen in the aircraft's doorway.

Crossair's first SF340 tucks up its landing gear on take-off from Lugano with Pope John aboard.

By August 1984, SF340 development aircraft had logged over 370 flight test hours. Here an unpainted third aeroplane, SE-ISB, takes-off for the first time on 25 August.

Having taken four SF340s into the air, their crews celebrated with this brief four-ship formation. From left to right are the first, fourth (Comair's N340CA), third (SE-ISB) and second aircraft.

While the first four SF340s were being put through their paces, the next nine production airframes were being assembled.

Waiting patiently in the snow for their passengers in pale winter sunshine are a pair of Norving Norway's Saab 340s. From November 1985 the aircraft became known by this name when Fairchild Industries left the SF340 Joint Venture programme.

'On finals'. The Captain and First Officer of this Northwest Airlink Saab 340 have a splendid view as the aircraft, at 150m (500 ft) is established on the centre line and half a mile from touch-down.

Passengers board a Northwest Airlink's Saab 340 - the 76th to be built - at a US regional airport.

This unique photograph, taken at Switzerland's Basle-Mulhouse Airport early in April 1986, shows what was then the entire Crossair fleet of Saab 340s.

On 23 February 1985, a Kendell Airlines Saab 340 arrived at its home base at Wagga Wagga, Australia, after a five day 18,900 km (10,200 miles) delivery flight from the Saab factory. Total flying time was 46 hours.

Serge Gregory, on the left, became the ten millionth Saab 340 passenger when he flew Air France from Paris to London on 9 September 1988 Saab Aircraft's Philip Male presented him with a souvenir of his historic milestone flight.

This photograph of an Air New Zealand Link Saab 340, and the next five, show the distinctive markings carried by a few of the many airlines which operate this very successful regional airliner.

China Southern carries a red lotus flower on its fin and its name in two languages...

... Japan Air Commuter favours an all-white finish with a bold black, yellow and red tail paint job...

... as does Air Baltic, with blue lettering and a dash of chequer board patterns...

... and KLM City Hopper's Saab 340B follows the same pattern with its complete tail unit a dark blue...

... while Sweden's Skyways, with giant red lettering on an all-white airframe, makes sure we know who we're flying with!

In complete contrast is this matt grey Airborne Early Warning Saab 340. It carries all the external gubbins for the Ericsson Erieye radar on its back, which makes it the world's most versatile, high performance, low cost AEW system.

'Down a bit': adding the pointed end of a Saab 340B to the rest of the fuselage. This aircraft was being built for Formosa Airlines.

A model of Saab's 2105 light-weight multi-role combat aircraft project. It beat foreign competitors to win a contract from Sweden's Defence Materiel Administration on 30 June 1982. The model is in ground attack configuration.

This full scale mock-up of the JAS 39A Gripen was first shown during a press briefing on 12 February 1986.

The first of five single-seat Gripen prototypes which was rolled out on 26 April 1987.

Stig Holmström, Saab's military chief test pilot, who first flew the Gripen.

'Here we go'. Stig Holmström takes the Gripen prototype into the air for the first time on 9 December 1988.

The second pre-production Gripen carrying rocket pods with wing tip Sidewinder air-to-air missiles.

This steeply banked Gripen shows five weapons or pod pylons, plus the bulged fairing over the 27 mm Mauser cannon.

A pair of Gripens with assorted external loads. The nearer aircraft has wingtip Sidewinders, a Falcon air-to-air missile, Rbs15F anti-ship missile and a centre line tank or pod.

Four of the five pre-production Gripens. Note the small horizontal vortex generating strakes where the pitot boom joins the nose.

The second production Gripen being built. Despite the advanced technologies and equipment involved in its design and construction, there is still a need for the inevitable tin can and small brush seen on the staging!

Gripen weapon load. From left to centre, back row: Rbs15F anti-ship missiles, DW539 submunitions dispenser, two rocket pods, drop tanks. Middle row: two Rb75 Maverick missiles. Front row: Skyflash and Sidewinder missiles.

This photograph shows many of the Gripen's design features: the foreplanes, air intakes, twin-wheel nose landing gear and the fuselage-mounted main gear units, plus the very large cockpit canopy.

The Gripen is designed for very rapid turn around time between missions by four conscripted Servicemen and a crew chief. Here the team load a guided missile beside a submunitions dispenser.

Saab 2000s being built for Third Millennium service. The lead aircraft carries the number six with, presumably, numbers seven to ten beyond it.

In a glistening white finish with three shades of blue around its tail end, the first Saab 2000, SE-001, stands ready for roll out.

Queen Silvia of Sweden gives her royal accolade to the first Saab 2000 by signing her name on its nose.

Up and away. The resplendent first Saab 2000 soars into the blue. The six swept composite blades of its Dowty propellers are very apparent.

Saab 2000 SE-001, its port side revealing Crossair livery, keeps company with an American Eagle airline Saab 320B.

The first three Saab 2000s. 'Wool tufts' are fixed to the starboard wing and tailplane and engine nacelle of the nearest aircraft and to the port wing and nacelle of the middle aircraft.

Ergonomics played a large part in the design of this ultra-modern flight deck of the Saab 2000.

The third prototype Saab 2000 over-flies Farnborough International '92. With few cars and no aeroplanes on the ground, this must have been a pre-show arrivals day photograph.

Photographed on the ground at Farnborough International '92, the Saab 2000's large 3.8 m (12 ft 6 in) diameter propeller dominates this view of the third aircraft.

In restyled Crossair livery the fourth aircraft is posed for the cameraman.

A bird's eye view of part of the Saab production facilities at Linköping, which have been progressively and extensively expanded.

124

Compared with most airlines Deutsche BA's livery strikes a more sombre note. This Saab 2000's number is 007. A James Bond special?

Ten aircraft later came these eye-catching tail-end markings from AIR Marshall Islands.

The red flying bird motif of France's Regional airline appears three times on this Saab 2000, on its nose, fuselage and tail.

Scandinavian Commuter Swelink puts its tri-national red, yellow and blue colours at the front of its Saab 2000 with the coats of arms of Sweden, Denmark and Norway at the rear end.

The appropriately-named Saab 9000 Aero motorcar of 1997, styled for the 50th Anniversary year...

... and the 1998 Saab 9-5, the car for the future.

No bright colour scheme for this Airborne Early Warning version of the Saab 2000 with Ericsson Erieye radar. As this photograph has 'Montage' stamped on it, it is in fact an artist's impression and not the real thing.